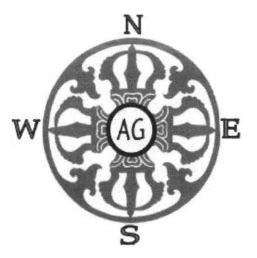

By

JOHN A WILLIAMS
& T.J. MILLER

THE LORDS OF ADVENTURE

ADVENTURER'S HANDBOOK

EXPANDED EDITION

BY JOHN A WILLIAMS & T.J. MILLER (AKA ~ JACK BOLD & ROGER AWESOME)

"CHOOSE TO BE A HERO, OR BE A VICTIM BY ACCIDENT."

Acknowledgements:

Special thanks to all those teachers who have contributed to helping me to become who I wanted to be. To mom & dad for always accepting and encouraging who I am even when you did not understand. To Calvin Martin, Bruce Wilshire & Doug Nason for opening my mind. Master Martin, Craig Stanton, Alex Wilkie & Rick Tucci for giving me the martial arts. To Bethany, Elise, Katrina, & Cheryl for helping me to understand what love is, and for loving me even when I did not deserve it. To Bruce Lee & Dan Inosanto for creating the philosophy that has changed my life. To all of my martial arts students, all of our amazing fans, and all the other teachers & angels who have shaped who I am today.

~T.J.

I'd like to thank all those adventurers who made my life the most exciting place to be. To my parents for giving me the freedom to follow my own path and for showing me that love is the most powerful force in the universe. To my Brother Bob and my sister Benita for knowing I was different from day one and loving me anyway. To my children Kayla and Jacob for being the reason I keep going. To my Ex-wife Leah for giving me the two best children on any planet and for still being my friend. To my Mende for being the air I breathe.

~John

What is an Adventurer?

The road of the adventurer is the path of the hero. This path is not for the faint of heart or the mild of constitution, for the adventurer follows the path of action. Scholars record the path, dreamers dream about the path, but the adventurer walks the path, always moving forward on the quest for a life of adventure and meaning.

If the choices are hope, and hopelessness, the adventurer chooses hope, even in the darkest hours. A true adventurer continues until the job is done. In a world of optimists and pessimists, who find their glasses half full or half empty, the adventurer is satisfied having a glass. The adventurer embraces the quest to find a drink to fill the vessel. Make no mistake, the adventurer will find a way to fill the glass.

An adventurer endeavors to become the master of the now. Understanding that life is fleeting and precious, the adventurer savors every moment as if it could be the last.

"Hoka Hey" ~ Sioux Indian blessing meaning: "it is a good day to die."

This blessing is not morbid, but a statement of freedom. Understanding how precious life is, the adventurer embraces the fact that each day could be the last one dancing in this great mystery of life and thus, lives each moment fully and with pure intent and heart.

The path of the adventurer is the path of the warrior, understanding his own mortality, he is not held captive by his or her fear, but embraces the utter freedom of a meaningful life, a life living itself *Boldly*, and each moment is *Awesome!*

"Know the path, then walk on."
~Larry Hartsell

"The basic difference between an ordinary man & an adventurer is that an adventurer takes everything as a challenge, while an ordinary man takes everything as a blessing or a curse."
~Paraphrase of Carlos Cataneda

THE ADVENTURER'S CODE

"An adventurer without a code is a wild beast loosed upon this world."

~Paraphrase of Albert Camus

The Adventurer's Code is the soul and spirit of an adventurer. To live by this code transforms one's life from a thing of mediocrity into a quest, into something epic, into an adventure. Every day is an adventure, and those who live by this code enhance and realize that adventure.

Hold fast to the code! Follow its teachings and edicts, and begin to walk the path of the hero.

THE ADVENTURER'S CODE

- ⊕ Always make a proper entrance
- ⊕ Get the ball rolling
- ⊕ When you act, act with confidence
- ⊕ Love deeply and without regret
- ⊕ Abandon regret & guilt
- ⊕ Live with Passion

Always Make a Proper Entrance

Make a proper entrance and the exit will be taken care of for you. Notice that the word here is "proper" entrance. The entrance does not always have to be "grand." A proper entrance is one in which the adventurer can assess the situation and respond accordingly. The evaluation of the situation may lead to the understanding that no entrance will be proper and the adventurer can leave to come back at another time.

The Adventurer strives to always know and choose their playing field or field of battle for the most advantage.

The greatest part of making an entrance is to have a proper assessment of the situation. This also involves knowing oneself and how you will respond in a situation. For example, it may not be the best time to discuss your relationship with a loved one if you had no sleep for three days or are in a horrible mood after a bad day at work.

If no proper entrance can be made, do not make one. Take a moment to breathe and regroup until you can make a proper entrance for the situation.

Get the Ball Rolling

"Today is the first day of the rest of your life."

~Charles Dederich

Understanding that each day we live could be our last dance here in this life, there is no time to lose. If you have something you have always wanted to do, some skill you have always wanted to learn, start! We fret away our lives, saving things for *"after"* or *"later."* Now is the day to begin learning that language you always wanted to know, to learn to play a musical instrument, to start eating better food, to exercise. In the arena of life, an adventurer does not waste time. The adventurer gets the ball rolling, knowing that in life, our number of heartbeats are limited and each day is lived as if it could be the last.

You can accomplish more with momentum. An object at rest tends to stay at rest; an object in motion tends to stay in motion. This principle is also true for human lives. Turn off the TV and MOVE!!!

When You Act,
Act with Confidence

"Whether you think you can, or you can't, you are right."

~Henry Ford

When the lion moves on the plains, every action is certain and determined. The other animals know that the king of the beasts is on the plain and they should take heed. The adventurer must act with the same confidence to reach full potential. When standing at a ravine, part of being able to make the jump to the other side is believing that you can. That was part of what Kierkegard meant by a leap of faith.

Be confident in what you do and believe in your inner adventurer and then that light and fire within will shine out to the world and you will move like a lion and not like prey or a victim.

"Nobody can make you feel inferior without your consent."

~Eleanor Roosevelt

Love Deeply & Without Regret

The heart is a muscle, the more it is exercised, the stronger it will become.

Love is not just a mushy feeling that happens in your stomach. Adventurers love deeply and feel passionately. Embrace these feelings, they are what make life beautiful and worth living. Feel what you feel, fully and deeply but be mindful of those you love. Our passion must be tempered with deep caring for others.

Love is not just a feeling. More importantly, love is a verb. To love something is to help it toward being the best that it can be. Love as an action and with honesty in your heart and thought.

We must temper our passions with the verb, the action of loving. If you truly love, you will help to lift the object of your love up to its full potential, helping your love on a journey to become the best he or she can be. Actual love is not about your ego, even though you will get more out of it than any other act of your life. To love is about the object of your love. True loving is selfless, and though its road may be hard, it is worth the walk.

"When love beckons to you, follow him, though his ways are hard and steep. And when his wings enfold

you yield to him, though the sword hidden among his pinions may wound you. And when he speaks to you believe in him, though his voice may shatter your dreams as the north wind lays waste the garden...
All these things shall love do unto you that you may know the secrets of your heart, and in that knowledge become a fragment of Life's heart."

~Kahlil Gibran

Abandon Regret & Guilt

"In a world where death is the hunter, my friend, there is no time for regrets or doubts. There is only time for decisions."

~Carlos Castaneda

Adventurers act. Living a life of clarity and purpose, once an adventurer makes a decision, they live with that decision understanding that the choice was born out of their very freedom. This is not to say that every decision an adventurer makes is correct, but heroes live with the consequences of their actions and learn from them. Adventurers do not deny their responsibilities.

Regret and guilt are debilitating. They can crush your soul. Adventurers have no time for this. Adventurers are not victims; they are the conscious, free creators of their world.

An adventurer cannot be free if they are in the shackles of doubt, regret and guilt.

Live with Passion

"Passion is universal humanity. Without it religion, history, romance and art would be useless."
~Honoré de Balzac

An adventurer lives and acts with passion. Every action has what the Greeks used to call *arête*, or excellence. Decide what you want and the kind of person you want to be and become it. Ignite the fire within you and allow yourself to become on fire for what you believe and the inner hero within will have no choice but to emerge.

This is the true essence of the Adventurer. All other things are contained within and made perfect in the forge of the adventurer's passion and zest for being excellent.

"You can have anything you want if you want it desperately enough. You must want it with an exuberance that erupts through the skin and joins the energy that created the world."

~Sheila Graham

THE
BE'S OF ADVENTURING

"I never had a policy; I have just tried to do my very best each and every day."

~Abraham Lincoln

Where the Adventurer's Code turns one's life from the mundane to the epic, the

Be's of Adventuring are the moral backbone of a life well lived. Anyone who follows the Adventurer's Code can be a hero, but without the Be's of Adventuring, the adventurer can just as easily be a villain.

All warrior societies had a code of conduct so that the warriors did not become tyrants. When you embrace the life of the adventurer, you will gain great power to affect your world. Follow the Be's of Adventuring and that power will be used for the greater good of everyone around you. An adventurer that follows the Be's will become a beacon of light in dark places for the whole family of humankind.

"With great power comes great responsibility."
~Uncle Ben from Spiderman

The Be's of Adventuring

⊕ Be!!!

⊕ Be Loving

⊕ Be Strong

⊕ Be Flexible

⊕ Be Bold

⊕ Be Awesome

⊕ Be Honest

⊕ Be in the Present

⊕ Be Who You Want to Be

⊕ Be Humble, Exude
   Confidence

Be!!!

Your very existence is a sacrament. Accept the magic of who you are and live it. There is already a Lord or Lady of Adventure living inside you.

     Of all the be's this is one of the most important. It is both the most simple and most complex. It is the basis for all other things. Many times in our complex modern world, we forget to just be who we are. We cannot help but to be, but yet we constantly fall into the tragedy of trying to be other than what we truly are. We try so hard to live up to other people's ideals of what we should be or some image that society tells us we should be, that we forget just how amazing we are.

     From the moment of your conception, you were already the best of millions of options, the winner of one of the greatest races in all of nature. You are a miracle. Your very existence is a sacrament. Accept your personal magic. Live the miracle that went into creating you. There is already a Lord or Lady of Adventure living inside you, it just needs your permission to show itself to the world.

"Never be bullied into silence. Never allow yourself to be made a victim. Accept no one's definition of your life; define yourself."

~Harvey Fierstein

Be Loving

"If you could only love enough, you could be the most powerful person in the world. "

~Emmet Fox

Of all the Be's of Adventuring, to be loving is probably the most powerful. All the great religions command us to love. Love can move mountains, Jesus said that we should have faith, hope and love, but that love was the greatest of the three. We talked earlier in the Adventurer's Code a little of what we believe of love and it is important that love is spoken of twice in this handbook.

What is the love that religions command of us? It cannot just be an emotion; one cannot be commanded to have a feeling. We speak here, as the religions of the world do, of the action of love. To be loving is to help someone or the world to be better than it is at this time. To love is to help something to grow beyond itself, to find its path and meaning.

Look at the world through the lens of love. Give up your ego in your actions and interactions with others. Do not be offended so easily and think of what people are trying to do to you, but look at them as the amazing forces of nature that they are. It is easy to do this with your friends, try to do it with those you do not like as well. Dealing with the world in this way can truly change your life, and the world.

"Love is a force more formidable than any other. It is invisible - it cannot be seen or measured, yet it is powerful enough to transform you in a moment, and offer you more joy than any material possession could."

"Love's greatest gift is its ability to make everything it touches sacred."

~Barbara de Angelis

<u>Be Strong</u>

"Strength does not come from winning. Your struggles develop your strengths. When you go through hardships and decide not to surrender, that is strength."

~Arnold Schwarzenegger

Be strong and resolute in your actions. Be strong in mind, body and spirit. As an adventurer you will be called upon to be a rock for others on occasion. Stand fast to what you believe and stand fast for those you love.

Do not be afraid of your strength. When you know what you believe in stand by it regardless of the opinions of others. It is also important to be strong in health and body as well. To be an adventurer is a total transformation of the self that includes the body as well as the mind. Create a diet and level of activity that will increase the strength of your health and body. Everything works together and your attitude will be more conducive to being a hero when you feel physically able.

We are all different; the level of strength we each achieve will be based on our own bodies. In the Adventurer's life, it is not a competition with anyone except yourself.

"To keep the body in good health is a duty, otherwise we shall not be able to keep our mind strong and clear."

~Buddha

Be Flexible

"Do not be tense, just be ready, not thinking but not dreaming, not being set but being flexible. It is being "wholly" and quietly alive, aware and alert, ready for whatever may come."

~Bruce Lee

While an adventurer must be strong of body, will and spirit, that strength is made perfect in flexibility. We learn all around us from nature that true strength and vitality must be flexible. The young sapling that is full of life will bend in the wind, but the old and dead tree will snap and break. The wings of a plane must be able to bend or they will snap.

The adventurer must be flexible and ready to adapt to any situation. I once heard a general tell my ROTC class that we needed to be steel. I knew that he was wrong. What we need to be is water. In an earthquake, our structures of steel and iron will snap and break, but the waters around us get a massage. If you are able to bend to new situations and ideas you will endure.

Be Bold

"Be bold. When you embark for strange places, don't leave any of yourself safely on shore. Have the nerve to go into unexplored territory."
~Alan Alda

Adventurers must go whole-heartedly into experiences. When you choose to act, act with your whole self. Put your full intention into everything you do. If it is worth doing it is worth doing boldly.

Do not be afraid to get out of your comfort zone and try new things. Put yourself out there and try new things. Even if you fail, we learn much more from our losses than we do from our defeats. Every defeat we suffer is an adventure in itself.

"We just got our butts kicked by the Knights of the Round Table. It was awesome!"

~Roger Awesome and Jack Bold

Be Awesome

"The question isn't who is going to let me; it's who is going to stop me."

~ Ayn Rand

Every one of us is a force of nature. Awesome is already burning inside you to get out and all you need to do is let it. An adventurer must embrace the excellence of what they are so they can shine that light on the world.

Work hard for everything you attempt and go into what you do as a hero because you are. You can be unstoppable.

31

Awesome people know that they can do whatever they wish to do. The answer is to believe that you can. If you truly believe it will happen.

Children know this. They are awesome all the time in their playing. Kids at play are super heroes and whatever else they want to be. We need to regain that childlike joy of life. We can be awesome because life itself is awesome, and we are a part of that whole great mystery of everything that is.

Approach everything you do as an awesome being. You are an adventurer; the mundane life is not good enough for you. You are epic and if you deal with the world as an epic and awesome force of nature, it will respond as such.

You will find that the universe answers whatever question you ask it. If you ask the universe, "Are you dangerous and out to get me?" The universe will tend to say "Yes. I am dangerous and out to get you." You can however change the question. Ask the universe instead, "Are you friendly and did you make me to be awesome?" The universe will tell you, and the answer will be so profoundly true that it will change your life, "Yes adventurer, I am friendly and you are indeed made to be awesome!" What question will you ask the universe?

Be Honest

"Be impeccable with your word. Speak with integrity. Say only what you mean. Avoid using the word to speak against yourself or to gossip about others. Use the power of your word in the direction of truth and love."   ~Miguel Ruiz

As an adventurer you must be honest, in both word and action. A great part of honor is following through with what you do, and taking responsibility for your actions. I once read of the samarai that they are honest not because it is the law of some divine being, but because to be dishonest is to be a coward. When we lie, we are afraid of the consequences of what we have done.

Many people in our world do not follow through. They will tell you what they think you want to hear and then change what was said when the time suits them. This happens often in business. A business partner will make promises so that they get what they want and then when the time comes to follow through, they claim that the deal was not what you thought. Do not be this person. Karma exists and the little bit you gain in that moment will be far less than what you will lose in trust and goodwill in the future.

When people know that you have integrity and are a person of your word, then you will receive trust in return. We truly reap what we sow, and if you put truth out to the world, truth will come back to you and it truly will set you free. Do nothing that you would be ashamed to tell someone that you truly respect after it is over. It is easy to be truthful when you live a life of virtue and are responsible for your actions.

"Honesty is the cornerstone of all success, without which confidence and ability to perform shall cease to exist."

~Mary Kay Ash

Be in the Present

"I have realized that the past and future are real illusions, that they exist in the present, which is what there is and all there is."

~Alan Watts

I once heard a preacher on a youth retreat sarcastically describe the typical way we go about planning for life in our modern society like this, "I have to stay in school and get good grades so I can go to the right college. Then I can get a good job so I can live in the right neighborhood and my kids can go to the right school, get good grades and go to the right college. Then they can get a good job and live in the right neighborhood so my grandkids can go to the right school..." We spend a great deal of time in our culture regretting the past or worrying about the future. It seems we are on a constant chase for some future reward. It is always that bigger office, or even reward in the afterlife that keeps us running the race and failing to notice what is happening in this moment. We take very little time to stop and smell the roses.

In reality, happily ever after happens now, a moment at a time. If your thought is constantly on the past and future you will miss all the glory of your life.

Being in the moment can also include being in the place where you actually are in today's technologically connected society. How often have you seen people at the mall or in an amusement park or out with friends texting or talking on the cell phone. We seem to have a great desire to be anywhere but where we are, whether it is where we are located in space, or when we are located in time.

Be where you are and be fully engaged. As an adventurer you can only achieve your maximum potential if you put your whole self into what you are doing. You can only have your full self in something if you are living Now.

Of course there will be times when you will reflect on the past or plan for the future. Most adventurers also use cell phones and the internet, but you need to try and practice making time to be here and now. Take a moment of pause every day to breathe deep and fully absorb everything around you. Watch the magic of life unfolding around you. If you are really ambitious do this for fifteen or twenty minutes. Maybe even go to a crowded place and watch life happening. Just concentrate on your breathing and quiet your mind. You will find that taking that small bit of time will make the rest of your day all the more productive.

Be Who You Want to Be

"Be who you are and say what you
feel, because those who mind don't
matter and those who matter don't
mind."

~Dr. Seuss

The whole of the code and the Be's of
Adventuring lead one inevitably to this
path. You must figure out who you want
to be and then become it. If you follow the
path of the adventurer you will achieve this
goal. There is no wrong answer to the
question of who you want to be, unless it is
not your own answer.

I remember sitting in the office of
an advisor in college and telling him how
much I enjoyed philosophy, but I was
afraid that I could not make a living with

that major. I asked him what he thought I should do and he gave me an answer that has changed my life to this day. "Who cares?" He told me that if I really enjoyed philosophy that I should make that my major and not to let those concerns stop me from studying what I was interested in. I stayed with it and it is one of the best decisions I have ever made.

The quality of life that I have enjoyed since then has been so much better because I became who I wanted to be and not something that I thought was more viable as a career. I have also found that I have always been able to work, and more, I have always enjoyed the work that I have done. Even more, I have never really thought of it as work.

Be Humble, Exude Confidence

"It was pride that changed angels into devils; it is humility that makes men as angels."

~Saint Augustine

We have noticed that quite often, especially with men, there is a great tendency to brag and make lofty claims about one's accomplishments. I have come to the point that when someone tells me the amazing things they have done, I tend to not believe them. I experience this many many times as someone who teaches the martial arts.

I have had people tell me that to pass their black belt test they were forced to fight twelve other black belts unarmed while the twelve wielded swords. Another man once told me that he and his friends would go into the woods, tie their hands together and knife fight. A student of mine when I was teaching high school told me that the style he studied was, "the illegal stuff." As someone with teachers who have done a lot of knife training and trying to learn the dangers of blades myself, I know these stories to be fiction. My teachers who are from the Philippines or have trained with those who are have the scars to prove it. Anyone who has done knife training knows that it is not something that you want to do and one against twelve in a knife fight equals dead. One against one with hands tied together equals West Side Story.

The funny thing about a lot of these people who tell tall tales about their exploits is that when you get to know them, they really do have amazing stories that are true. Most of them would not need to make up stories because their real stories are awesome! These people are adventurers already, but they lack humility, because they are really not that confident.

Most bragging comes from a place of insecurity and failure to realize all the things about oneself that we have talked about throughout this handbook. You are amazing and we all have had our share of adventures. You do not need to make up stories. Just be amazing like you are.

Let your actions speak for you and not your mouth. The fact is, that most people who go on and on about how amazing they are usually are not believed. Be an amazing expression of yourself and then you will never have to tell anyone. They will see you shine and recognize the adventurer that lives inside you, the adventurer that you are.

"When you were born, you cried and the world rejoiced. Live your life so that when you die, the world cries and you rejoice."

~Cherokee Saying

THE
ADVENTURER'S GUILD

"No man is an island entire of itself;
every man is a piece of the continent,
a part of the main."

~John Donne

What is the Adventurer's Guild?

The Adventurer's Guild is a journey. It can be an aid to releasing one's inner Lord or Lady of Adventure. It is a group of fans of the Lords of Adventure show. The Adventurer's Guild is fun, but it also may be a chance to begin a journey toward a healthier and more fulfilling life. The steps of the path through the Guild are suggestions that we feel can be powerful life changing quests and adventures for you on your personal quest.

Even though the various levels of the Guild have requirements and goals, ultimately the Adventurer makes his or her own path. Adventurers are not cut from a mold, they are individuals, and a Master Adventurer needs no one to provide goals or quests. The Master Adventurer makes their own adventures and could indeed write their own handbook that would be specific to their own personal journey.

Level 1 – "The Novice"
Adventure Guild Pin

Novice Level is the place where it all begins. The desire and will to be on the path makes one an adventurer. Remember to enjoy the process and see each level as amazing. It is the journey and not the destination that counts.

The symbols that make the arms of the compass in the Adventurer's Guild symbol are lotus flowers. Those seeds start in the muck and the mud and grow into some of the most beautiful flowers. This is a good analogy for what one becomes as an adventurer. Through all of the trials and hardships life throws at us, we emerge better than we were before, and armed with new knowledge, we follow the path of adventure.

"One step at a time, walk the thousand mile road."

~Musashi

The Quests to achieve "Novice" Level:

I.   Acquire an Adventurer's Guild Pin
II.   Let the Lords of Adventure know that you want to join the Guild and embrace the path of the Adventurer

Level II – "The Apprentice"
Wooden Medallion

At the level of Apprentice, the adventurer begins to practice what it takes to have adventures. At this level you actually have to do something aside from just state your desire to be an adventurer.

You will get as much out of this journey as you put in. When deciding on your adventure, challenge yourself. Maybe the place you decide to go will be a mountain top you have seen pictures of, or a secluded beach you read about in a magazine. Maybe you will go and see an artist you have always admired perform. The choice is yours. Be creative and realize this is your journey. You should enjoy your quest. We can't wait to hear what you come up with.

The Quests to achieve "Apprentice" Level:

I.   Be recognized as a Level I
        Adventurer

II.   Acquire an Adventurer's
        Handbook

III.   Complete Novice Quest #1

    a. Complete the "Hero's Quest." We can send it to you online or if you happen to be at a show we are performing at, you can get a copy there.

    b. Go to a place you've never been before on an adventure. This should be a place you've always wanted to go and get a picture of yourself there. Show it to one of the Lords of Adventure or send it to us on the internet.

Level III – "The Journeyman"
Bronze Medallion

The Journeyman continues to harness his or her inner adventurer and hone it in the fires of personal will. The quests here begin to get more intense and are geared toward making the adventurer better than they were before they embarked on this journey.

"An acorn is not an oak tree when it is sprouted... it has to endure all that frost and snow and side striking winds can bring before it's a full grown oak tree. These are rugged teachers, but rugged schoolmasters make rugged pupils. So a man is not a man when he is created, he is only begun."

~Henry Ward Beecher

The Quests to achieve "Journeyman" Level:

I.   Be recognized as a Level II Adventurer

II.   Make a list of your everyday adventures that you already do to better yourself (for example: working out, martial arts, scouting, practicing music, volunteering, learning to juggle, hiking, having a healthy breakfast, etc...) If you cannot think of anything you are already doing, choose some.

III.   Perform one every day adventure 5 days a week for a month.

IV.   Make a list of life goals (for example: Earn a Black Belt, Get your BA, Become an Eagle Scout, Join the Peace Corps, Backpack in Europe, Hike the Appalachian Trail, Start Your Own Business, etc...)

Level IV – "The Adventurer"
Silver Medallion

"It's easy to be a holy man on the top of a mountain."

~Bill Murray from <u>The Razor's Edge</u>

When one has achieved the level and title of Adventurer, we begin to move the focus away from honing the adventurer personally, and start to embark on how the adventurer interacts with, and makes the world a better place.

The Quests to achieve "Adventurer" Level:

I. Be recognized as a Level III Adventurer

II. Perform one of each of the following acts and let us know what you did:

a. Love: (Perform an act that loves the world around you

as a verb. Maybe work in a soup kitchen or help an elderly person with their groceries.)

b. Honesty: (Come clean with yourself about something bad you have done and make amends with the proper people.)

c. Flexibility: (Make a compromise with someone you disagree with and try to do it their way. Maybe this is someone you are in a relationship with or a coworker who sees something differently than you do.)

III. Pick a food or a vice that you really enjoy that may be bad for you, and give it up for a month. This is a great time to give up smoking or another bad habit. This could also be something like watching TV.

IV.   Develop a plan for and be on
        your way to achieving one of
        your life goals that you listed to
        achieve   the   rank   of
        Journeyman.

Level V – "The Veteran"
Gold Medallion

The Veteran adventurer is becoming
a serious force for change, in their own
lives and in the world around them. The
quests for Veteran status allow the
adventurer to take a serious look at the
positive people and events that have shaped
who the adventurer is, and to appreciate
those teachers of their personal journey.

It is also time to achieve one of the
bigger life goals that were set and thought
about at the earlier levels.

The Quests to achieve "Veteran" Level:

I.   Be recognized as a Level IV Adventurer

II.   Achieve one of your life goals to your satisfaction. If the goal is something like earning a black belt, it is pretty clear if it is done, but if it is something like playing a musical instrument, you need to be honest with whether or not you are happy with your skill level.

Make a timeline of important positive events of your past and realize how they shaped the person you are now (These may include an amazing trip or meeting a mentor for example.)

Thank three of the people from your timeline who helped teach you and helped make you who you are today.

Level VI – "Master Adventurer"
Bone Medallion

Master Adventurers make their own way. Once you achieve this level, we bow to you. You have succeeded at that which is not easy to do. Be proud of yourself and hold to the ways of the adventurer's path. Take what you have learned about yourself and the others around you and go forth and be a positive force in the world. We are happy to call you a brother or sister Master Adventurer. Carry on.

"Study strategy over the years and achieve the way of the adventurer. Today is your victory over self of yesterday. Tomorrow is your victory over lesser men."
~paraphrase of Myamoto Musashi

The Quests to achieve "Master" Level:

I.   Be recognized as Level V Adventurer

II. Go back to your timeline and add negative events of your past and list the important ones.

III. From your list, think of some trait in you that affects you negatively. Be honest. Let that trait go.

IV. Honestly forgive three people who have harmed you in some way, let them know only if you wish.

V.   Achieve another life quest, decided by you and the Lords of Adventure. This may be writing your own Adventurer's Handbook with your personal code and Be's of Adventuring that are important to you. This may be opening a small business. This may be

something that we have never
thought about. We can help you
decide.

Ending Statement

Thank you for taking this journey with us. We believe in the power of positive thinking and changing your life for the better. When you begin this journey, the desire to begin it is fuel in itself. To become an adventurer and accomplish all of the quests in this book is difficult; as are all things that are valuable in this journey we call life.

This handbook is one of our personal quests that John and I have been working on for many years. We learned from each other and from people we have met while performing, that being positive and embracing your inner adventurer can change your life, but more importantly it can change the world around you. We have seen the magic in the faces of our fans, both children and adults, as they experience our joy and energy that we strive every day to bring to our show.

This book is a labor of love and we want you all to know that we believe in you. We honestly believe that every one of you have the inner fire and beauty to become a light to the world around you. If you have been to one of our shows, you have already been a light to us.

We are also here for you. If you have any questions about the quests in this book, ask us. The quests we have come up with are loose guidelines, if you have an idea for your own quest, ask us and we will tell you what we think. The Adventurer's Guild, if you choose to try it, is your journey, not ours. Enjoy the journey and we are here if you need us. We honestly mean that, let us know if you have any questions or just want someone to talk to.

Many kind regards and much love,
The Lords of Adventure ~
T.J. Miller & John Williams

Contact:

Visit our website:
www.lordsofadventure.com
Email: lordsofadventure@gmail.com
And find us on facebook

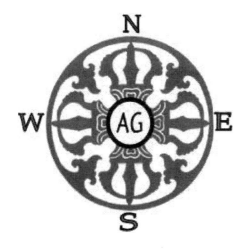

"Your life is your life
don't let it be clubbed into dank
submission. Be on the watch.
There are ways out.
There is a light somewhere.
It may not be much light but
it beats the darkness.
Be on the watch.
The gods will offer you chances.
Know them. Take them.
You can't beat death but you can
beat death in life, sometimes.
And the more often you learn to do
it, the more light there will be.
Your life is your life.
Know it while you have it.
You are marvelous
the gods wait to delight in you."

~Henry Charles Bukowski

Your Own Adventure Begins

Personal Notes:

Made in the USA
Middletown, DE
26 July 2024